I ♥ The Jonas Brothers

Harlee Harte

DOVE
BOOKS

I ♡
The Jonas Brothers

Dove Books has no affiliation with the title celebrity, and this book is not affiliated with or endorsed by the title celebrity. Harlee Harte and all surrounding characters and events are purely fictional. Any similarity with any real person is purely coincidental.

Copyright © 2009 Dove Books, Inc.

All rights reserved. Written permission must be secured from the publisher to use or reproduce any part of this book, except brief quotations in critical reviews and articles.

The opinions expressed in this book are those of the author of this book and do not necessarily reflect the views of the publisher or its affiliates.

ISBN-10: 1-59777-641-6
ISBN-13: 978-1-59777-641-7
Library of Congress Cataloging-In-Publication Data Available

Cover & Book Design by Sonia Fiore

Printed in the United States of America

Dove Books, Inc.
9465 Wilshire Boulevard, Suite 840
Beverly Hills, CA 90212

10 9 8 7 6 5 4 3 2 1

Collect all four
Harlee Harte books

I ♡ Taylor Swift

I ♡ The Jonas Brothers

I ♡ Selena Gomez

I ♡ Robert Pattinson

Hi!

I'm Harlee Harte.

I write the celebrity column, "HarteBeat," for the Hollywoodland High School newspaper. It's a blast! I get to meet and greet the hottest teen idols and hit the hip Tinseltown places to hang out and shop while I'm on the hunt. Being a columnist is hard work, but I just love the glamour and excitement! I'm always looking for the latest news about our favorite stars, so visit my Facebook page and see what I have going on or just say hello. My friends Kiki, Marcy, and Luzie pop in every now and then, too, and love to chime in on the latest fashions, cool beauty tips, music, celeb sightings, and advice on how to deal with parents, school, crushes, and friends.

I'd love to hear from you!

Harlee Harte

TABLE OF CONTENTS

PART ONE The Assignment

PART TWO The Column

PART THREE Games & Quizzes

PART ONE
The Assignment

"I can't believe I'm going to be late again! Gotta go!"

I flipped my phone shut, leaving Kiki in the middle of some unfinished whispered revelation. I could just see Kiki, Miss Fashion of Hollywoodland High, standing there in her skinny jeans and heels, holding her pink-cased iPhone with an annoyed look. I would have laughed, but being late to homeroom was not a laughing matter.

I hustled to Room 201, slinking through the door just after the late bell rang. I slid quietly into my chair, sitting there still as stone with my book bag still over my shoulder, legs in the aisle. I didn't move an inch. I could have been a statue in Madame Tussauds Wax Museum. *That still.* Maybe Mr. Thomas, sitting at his desk correcting papers, would not see me...

"Harlee Harte. That's the third time this week," Mr. Thomas said, without lifting his head.

I ♡ The Jonas Brothers

"Detention is next on your agenda. Perhaps a student celebrity reporter such as yourself would find a story worth writing about in detention. A story on the more, how should I put this, *realistic* side of life. It might increase the readership of the student newspaper which is usually, I am told, used to swat flies in the lunchroom. What do you think?"

Mr. Thomas was now standing right next to me. *That always freaks me out.* Can't he just wait for my answer at his desk?

"Well, you never know," I answered flippantly. "There may be a celebrity there. They get detention too. I know because…"

"That wasn't the answer I wanted, Harlee." He loomed over me, huge hands on my desk, and stared me in the face. I lowered my eyes. It was bad enough to have him for homeroom, but I had to face him later in history.

I was squirming now. *Had I pushed Mr. Thomas over the edge?*

All of a sudden there was a squeal and a squawk, and Mrs. Marshall, our slightly batty, stuck-in-the-'70s principal, burst through the PA system. "Good morning, Stars! Welcome to the start of another productive, challenging week of school. Before I get to the SAT schedule and club updates, I am happy to tell you all that on Saturday we will be having a dance in the gym, thanks to the organizing efforts of the Pep Club. It's going to be a Turnabout...girls will ask the boys this time. What fun! Now, all juniors signed..."

Girls ask boys? The whole room was buzzing. Girls were whispering conspiratorially; several hunks were showing off their muscles. Whatever Mrs. Marshall was saying about the SAT schedule was lost in the noise. But I just had one thought as Mrs. Marshall droned on: *Could I ever get up the nerve to ask my crush, the ever-so-hot and handsome Jack Kelly?*

Mr. Thomas called the room to order, but the first period bell rang, and the excited chatter

I 💟 The Jonas Brothers

spilled out into the hall. I had barely exited the classroom when I was accosted by my three BFFs: Marcy, Luzie, and Kiki.

I couldn't help notice how cute Luzie looked in her baby-blue Stars' varsity soccer jersey. *She must have a game today.* And tall, slightly awkward Marcy had a retro hippie headband on and sandals. *OMG...it didn't seem to work with the fake nose ring and henna tattoos...but that's Marcy.* I was sure Kiki would have something to say about that fashion faux pas, but instead she zeroed in on me.

"Thanks for hanging up on me," Kiki said with a petulant tone, then added, "I like your skirt."

"Oh, I picked it up at H & M in the mall. They have other colors too and matching..."

"You guys, can we dispense with the fashionista routine? Hello...there's a dance, and for like the first time *ever*, we get to ask the guys!" Marcy exclaimed.

"I'm asking Joey at lunch," Luzie said calmly, fingers working her iPod playlist, earphones already in her ears. "I gotta fly. I promised to help hang up posters for the dance." She waved happily to us and disappeared into the fast-moving crowd.

Of course she's asking Joey...he's her boyfriend. If she weren't so cute, I could really be jealous right now.

"Are you going to ask Jack?" Kiki asked.

"This is the perfect opportunity," Marcy added.

"Uh...I don't know. He barely speaks to me. I'm not sure he's into me," I answered.

"Oh, you worry too much. It's just a dance. Ask him," Kiki ordered. "What's the worst case scenario? He'll say no?"

He'd say no? That would be way more than a worst case scenario. That would be like a total-Titanic disaster.

"I'm asking Zack," Marcy said. "If I can do it, you can."

I ♥ The Jonas Brothers

Zack was Marcy's crush from her poetry class. Oddly, though they never really talked to each other or hung out, there was something in the way they looked at each other, especially when no one was paying attention...except me. *A good reporter sees things other people don't notice.*

"You totally should ask him, Marcy," Kiki offered, "since you two have googly-eyes for each other."

She noticed too? I should never underestimate ever-vigilant Kiki.

Both of my friends were staring at me, waiting for me to say something about asking Jack.

But I didn't know if I could ask Jack...or that I should even ask him if I could. I was feeling the pressure. Kiki was tapping her foot impatiently. Marcy was smiling in anticipation. I was getting really stressed out. Suddenly the first late bell rang. I was literally saved by the bell! It was the first time I actually liked the sound.

Marcy and Kiki rushed off in different directions. Kiki, heels clacking, yelled over her shoulder, "We'll talk about this at lunch!"

Like right. I didn't know if I wanted to talk about it at lunch. I wasn't ready.

I gathered my wits about me when I realized I was standing in the nearly empty hall. I rushed toward the gym. *PE on top of everything else*. At least I was in an all-girl class. But then...the dance would be all they talk about. There was no escaping it.

I rounded the corner full speed ahead, envisioning drill-sergeant Miss Swenson making me do laps for being late, when I crashed into another human being with a loud smack.

"Oh, excuse me, I'm so sorry. I wasn't looking where..."

I froze. My apology stuck in my throat, blocking my airway, when I caught a whiff of a familiar scent...Polo Blue. I looked up. *I had run right into Jack!*

I ♡ The Jonas Brothers

"No worries," I heard him say, as I stood there like the wordless wonder.

But Jack did not run off. He hesitated as if he were waiting for me to say something.

I turned beet red when I noticed we were standing right under a poster that read:

THE FIRST-EVER HOLLYWOODLAND HIGH TURNABOUT DANCE

Saturday, 8 p.m.—In the Gym

GIRLS, DON'T BE SHY! ASK YOUR CRUSH TODAY!

Aaagh!

Recovering quickly, I shifted my book bag on my shoulder, and smiling brightly, said, "I'm late to PE, see ya later."

And off I flew. I looked over my shoulder and saw Jack standing there watching me leave. Was that kind of a disappointed look on his face? *No. I must be imagining things. Maybe at lunch I could say something, laugh about our crash, mention the poster, back my way into asking him.... Yes! That could work.*

I had a plan.

The lunchroom...

I grabbed a tray and utensils and started down the lunch line. I could see Kiki, Luzie, and Marcy already seated at our table. Sondra, Hollywoodland High's very own Beverly Hills, BMW-driving, Prada-baby, was headed their way smiling. I saw Kiki cross her arms as Sondra started talking. *Not a brain in her bleached-blonde head, but Sondra sure could turn heads.*

I looked around for Jack but couldn't spot him. I was so ready to ask him to the dance. I had practiced my lines over and over while doing my punishment laps in PE, and I felt prepared and confident.

I ♥ The Jonas Brothers

Just then Philip Pendleton IV came up behind me in line. The editor in chief of the *Hollywoodland Star*, he never ceased to annoy me with his fake Harvard accent and arrogant way. And those tweedy blazers with elbow patches. *Gimme a break.*

I looked around. There was no way to avoid him. Then I had an idea. I would butt into the conversation two freshman girls were having in line in front of me about the Jonas Brothers. I knew that impeccably-mannered Philip would be too polite to interrupt.

"I think Joe is the cutest. He's funny too," said a petite blonde with braces.

"I like Nick best...he's so cute, and he can really sing," her Asian friend said, pushing her glasses up on her nose.

Here was my chance:

"Well, Kevin is the one for me. I'd date him in a heartbeat," I said.

"Duh...he's engaged," the little blonde said sarcastically.

Both of them turned their backs on me and snickered. I thought I heard something like, "some celebrity reporter" but I wasn't sure.

Philip cleared his throat. "Harlee, we're putting the paper to bed early next week because of Spring Break, so you can't be late with your column...as is your usual habit," Philip said.

"Don't lose any sleep over it, Philip. I'll have it for you on Wednesday morning, first period," I said. "You can count on me."

"Fine. I mean, that would be great," Philip said, stammering. Then he added casually, "I suppose you're going to the dance Saturday." His voice cracked on the word "Saturday."

"I'm planning on it," I replied cheerily. *If I could only get away from you to ask Jack!*

"Oh, well..," Philip responded in a flat tone, "then...could you do a blurb on it for the paper?"

"I guess so. Sure, why not?" All of a sudden I spotted Jack. He was dumping his tray and getting ready to leave.

I ♡ The Jonas Brothers

"Here, hold this," I said as I shoved my tray into Philip's hands and left him standing there as I hurried toward Jack.

I called out to Jack, and he turned around. I caught up to him and said, "Do you have a minute?"

"Sure," Jack smiled and pushed his hair away from his blue eyes. "As long as you're standing still this time."

"Oh, I'm sorry about that. I was in such a hurry...and I was late *anyway!*"

As I was talking I could see Kiki and Marcy waving at me wildly, and a very determined Luzie was making a beeline toward me through the tables as if she were pushing a soccer ball down the field. *Giving me encouragement. What great friends!*

But I didn't need any. In fact, much to my surprise, I threw my script aside and just blurted out:

"Jack, do you wanna go to the dance with me on Saturday?"

23

There was a heart-stopping silence. It was as if the whole room suddenly froze, and all eyes were on me.

Jack answered, "Harlee.... Gee, I'm sorry. Sondra just asked me."

Sondra?

Suddenly it all clicked into place in one horrifying epiphany:

Sondra smiling, talking to Kiki, Marcy, and Luzie.

Kiki's crossed arms.

Luzie trying to head me off.

Kiki's and Marcy's wild waves and gestures.

They weren't encouraging me. They were trying to *stop* me.

I looked at Jack with my mouth open.

"Are you okay?" he asked.

"Yeah. Sure. See you around, Jack."

I bolted to the girls' room with my three BFFs close behind.

I ♡ The Jonas Brothers

After school...

I didn't meet up with Marcy and Kiki at our bench outside school in the courtyard, and I didn't say good luck to Luzie as she boarded the bus for her away game.

I just started walking straight home. I was talked out.

My cell was ringing, and text messages were chiming in, but I didn't want to have any more reminders of the colossal blunder I had made. I wanted to go to my room and hide. Suddenly, I heard my name being called, and my neighbor, Toby, whom I've known since we were five, caught up to me.

"Hey, Harlee. What's up?" Toby asked innocently. "Here give me your book bag. It looks like it weighs a ton." Toby didn't wait for a reply, just relieved me of the bag and slung it over his shoulder with ease.

Toby is the ultimate California-surfer poster boy: spiked sun-bleached blond hair, blue eyes, muscular, and tan. Girls at the beach go crazy for him, but I don't get it—to me he is just little Toby, squirting me with his water pistol.

"Are you going to the dance Saturday?" Toby asked. "I mean, did you ask someone?"

"I don't know," I said, trying to save face as Toby apparently hadn't heard about my "most embarrassing moment."

Then I had a thought. *Toby.* Why not? Everyone knows we're just old friends. Asking him would seem natural. It would solve the problem. And he would go with me.

"Maybe I'll go. You wanna go with?" I asked as nonchalantly as I could.

Toby stopped walking. He looked at me with a worried face and said, "Har, Kiki asked me, and I said yes. I woulda gone with you, you know that. But I thought you'd ask Jack."

Oh great. Do I tell him I did ask Jack and that he's the backup guy? No way.

I ♥ The Jonas Brothers

"Oh. You'll have fun with Kiki. She's great," I said with a weak smile.

Toby handed me my book bag, and I ran inside my house. I peeked out the window and saw Toby still standing there. In a minute he turned and left. I slumped against the door. *What a day!*

That night...

I was setting the table for dinner while my mom made a salad, when my dad barreled through the kitchen door with my little brother Alec in tow. I wasn't in the mood for troublemaker, eight-year-old Alec, that was for sure, so I hoped he would have the good sense to stay out of my way.

But he ran right up to me and pointed to a medal pinned to his chest. "Look, Harlee, I'm the third grade 'bassdoor.'" Then he ran to mom to show it off.

"Ambassador," Dad corrected. "You are the third grade ambassador, which means you represent the third grade to the public on Pride Night."

"I'm proud of you, Alec. I know you will do a great job," Mom said, hugging him. "Tinseltown Elementary Pride Night is a lot of fun. I'm helping with refreshments."

"And I'm setting up some awesome games," Dad added.

"Are you going to come too, Harlee?" Alec asked, polishing his medal with his grubby little hand.

"Not if I can help it," I said, not too nicely.

"Harlee," Mom said, "we all turned out for you when you were little. Perhaps it would be a good idea if you did help out. That is, of course, if you don't have any other plans for Saturday night."

Saturday night? Wait. Was this my way out of an embarrassing situation? I had to help out at Pride Night. I couldn't get out of it. A family thing. Have to miss the dance...can't ask anyone. So sad.

I ♥ The Jonas Brothers

"You're right, Mom," I said sincerely. "I'd be happy to help out."

"That's great, Harlee! I have the perfect job for you. You can run the raffle. The Sullivans were going to do it, but they had to cancel."

Dad smiled, Alec hugged me, and Mom grabbed the phone to tell the raffle committee chairwoman she had a volunteer. There was no turning back now.

Raffle here I come.

Later that night...

"I know. It's a bummer," I said to Kiki, as I sprawled on my purple and pink bed with a stack of celebrity magazines, some pita chips, and my cell phone.

"Yeah. I have to be there at seven. There's no way I can get out of it. The 'rents won't hear of it, trust me."

Kiki babbled on about the dance and what she was going to wear. I wanted to tell her that Toby likes a natural look, but, hey, it was Kiki, and Kiki has her own distinct style. Toby would just have to go with the flow.

"Are you okay?" Kiki suddenly asked. "About Jack? About what happened today, I mean."

"Sure," I responded, kicking off my pink Converse. "As it turns out, I would have had to tell him I couldn't go anyway. It's fine."

I didn't really feel that way, of course, but the cover-up was working, and I was getting out of a bad situation gracefully. My friends would tell everyone about the raffle, and soon the whole school would know that I was busy Saturday night with family obligations. No one would wonder why I wasn't at the dance.

Perfecto.

The next day...

When I woke up, I put a heating pad on my forehead for a minute then jumped back into bed, hiding the heating pad under my pillow.

I ♡ The Jonas Brothers

"Mom...I don't feel good. I think I have a fever," I yelled.

Mom came in and felt my head. "Oh, it does look like your running a little fever. There's a virus going around. You'd better stay home today."

Score! But just then Alec came bounding into my room and jumped on my bed. He spotted the heating pad and pulled it out from under the pillow. "What's this? Wowee...it's hot!" he yelped as he tossed it on the floor.

Mom picked it up. I was busted. "Harlee, really. Get ready for school and don't be late."

Alec stuck his fingers in his ears and wagged his tongue at me. I threw my pillow at him, and he left, yelling, "Mommy, Harlee threw her pillow at me!"

What a great start to what would probably be a totally wretched day.

At school...

I was trying to close my locker, but it was like an unseen force was pushing from the other side. I put my shoulder into it with no luck. It wasn't like there was nonessential stuff in there. *Why wouldn't it close?*

I opened the locker and started to take some things out. I had almost an entire second wardrobe, my makeup and costumes left over from the last three years of class plays, one shin guard, a deflated basketball, three pairs of shoes that weren't mine, yellow rubber boots borrowed from Marcy, and an umbrella or two. Oh, and there was my camera. I had been looking all over for it. I did some rearranging and tried again.

No luck! Suddenly an arm appeared over my head and slammed the locker shut. I turned around to thank the person. It was Jack.

"Oh, thanks, Jack. I guess I'll have to clean this locker out sometime," I managed to get out.

"Bring a truck," he said deadpan.

"Come on, it's not that bad," I replied, smiling.

Then I said something really dumb. The words just rushed out of my mouth in a slightly hysterical torrent:

I 💛 The Jonas Brothers

"You know, I asked you to the dance...'cause I had to write a story about it for the school newspaper and needed a date.... Philip asked me to write it, and I couldn't say no. You just can't say no to him, he gets all uppity...and then, as it turns out, I have to volunteer at my little brother's school with my whole family...Pride Night...so I wouldn't have been able to go anyway, and...so it's good you're going with Sondra."

As soon as I finished I wished I could have plucked all those words out of the air and put them back in my big mouth. But the deed was done, so I braced myself for Jack's response. But before Jack could utter a word, Kiki and Marcy came rushing up to me, crowding around me, pulling me away.

"Harlee, come on! Mrs. Marshall wants to see us in her office. Hurry up!" Kiki said as she grabbed my arm. "We're in big trouble."

"But...what did we do?"

"Nothing! But someone scribbled graffiti all over our bench...and used our names!" Marcy exclaimed as she pushed me along.

33

I looked back to say goodbye to Jack, but he was already walking down the hall.

At the bench...

I was busy scrubbing away at the graffiti on our bench in the courtyard with some special cleaner the janitor gave me. I had sent Luzie off to get some more cleaning rags, while Kiki and Marcy went to get us all some lunch.

I was pretty content with myself, except for my rather pathetic attempt to convince Jack of my false intentions. That definitely did not come out the way I expected, and I wondered what he must have thought of me. But on the brighter side of things, I had passed around my excuse for missing the dance (making sure Sondra knew it and would question whether she was, in some twisted around way, second banana), avoided Philip Pendleton IV who was bugging me about the subject of next week's celebrity column, and even chatted up Mr. Thomas about Pride Night and volunteering.

I 💜 The Jonas Brothers

Kiki and Marcy came up loaded with drinks and sandwiches. They plopped down on the ground next to the defaced bench.

"I'm getting my hair done for the dance," Marcy said, biting into a veggie sandwich. "Maybe I should get highlights."

"I still haven't figured out what to wear," Kiki said, wrinkling up her nose as she picked apart her sandwich. "I saw a really cute tee at Kitson...but I don't know."

"Well, I don't have to worry about it," I laughed, as Luzie came into view with the rags in one hand and Joey hanging on to her other one.

"Hi, Joey!" I said. Joey is just perfect for Luzie. He smiles all the time and has a great way about him, plus he is an athlete like her. The only problem is that he and Luzie talk in Spanish a lot, and, although I'm taking Spanish, I'm never sure what they are saying! But Luzie assures me it's all good!

"Que pasa, ladies?" Joey said, giving high-fives all around. "Need some help?"

I handed Joey the smelly cleaner, and he went right to work. With some muscle behind it, the bench was starting to look good. Then Toby came up and asked Joey, "What are you doing, bro?"

"Cleaning the grafitti off. This stuff is really cool."

"Hey, let me try," Toby said, and I handed him some rags. Now we had two guys scrubbing the bench!

Just as I bit into my sandwich, Philip came into view. *So much for avoiding him.*

"Who messed up the bench? Maybe we should do a story on school vandalism," Philip suggested.

"Or not," I said. Toby and Joey snickered.

"So you're not going to the dance, I hear," Philip said. "Who's going to cover it for the paper?"

"Why don't you do it? You can go solo," I suggested. "Or better yet, ask Sondra to do it . She's going, and she's been begging for an assignment, right?"

I ♡ The Jonas Brothers

"I might just do that," Philip said with conviction.

"You may regret that, Philip," Marcy said. "Sondra's in my English class. She asked Mrs. Lewiston what a verb was yesterday. And she wasn't kidding."

Kiki and Luzie suppressed giggles as I choked on my sandwich.

Philip shook his head and walked away. I sighed with relief. He didn't ask me about the column. I guess we distracted him! But the reality was I had no clue who to write about. With this whole dance fiasco, I hadn't given it any thought. Plus there didn't seem to be an interesting celeb within fifty miles this week.

Uh, oh. Just then, Philip Pendleton IV turned around and strode purposefully right back up to me. I, once again, had a mouthful of sandwich.

"I meant to ask you yesterday, before being dumped holding your tray, whom are you choosing to write about this week?" Philip asked.

I could see Toby and Joey mouthing "dumped" but I resisted the urge to laugh and answered, "Well, Philip, let me put it this way: I have like absolutely, totally, no earthly clue."

This sent everyone into spasms, and Philip retreated in a hurry, throwing his arms up in the air in a dramatic display of frustration. *For a moment, just a fleeting moment, I felt sorry for him.* I dug my phone out of my bag and texted him:

Me: see u 18tr re celeb need ur help

Philip: Okay. We can meet in the library after 8th period and brainstorm.

I flipped my phone shut and had to laugh. Philip was the only person I knew who texted in full sentences, with complete punctuation!

Just as I was feeling really good about the day, I spotted Sondra walking with Jack across the courtyard. She was walking real close to him, and,

I ♡ The Jonas Brothers

worse yet, they seemed to be having a fun conversation.

Kiki followed my solemn gaze. "Hey, don't worry. She probably said something dumb, and he's just laughing at her."

I wish.

In the library...

Philip was waiting for me when I finally got to the library, hauling a huge bag of stuff from my locker. I was already exhausted, and I only went about one hundred feet!

I sat down across from him at the table and pulled out my notebook and pen.

"Hold on.... I asked Sondra to join us. She has some good ideas," Philip said.

I was furious. Without a word, I started packing up my stuff.

"Where are you going? Philip asked. "She'll be here in a minute."

"And I won't be," I retorted.

And with as much dignity as I could muster, while dragging a bag of locker leftovers, I left the library and never looked back, though I imagined Philip was once again throwing his arms up in exasperation.

By the time I dragged myself and the tattered garbage bag of junk all the way home, I was exhausted. Naturally, when I really needed Toby's help, he was nowhere around.

I went straight to my room and plopped on my bed. As my eyes closed, thoughts swirled through my head: *Got to find a celeb for the column next week. But who? How did I mess up so badly with Jack? The dance. Jack and me. Jack and Sondra.*

Jack and me...

Saturday night...

Mom dropped me off in an empty room at Tinseltown Elementary with folding chairs stacked

I ♡ The Jonas Brothers

to the ceiling on one side. What was I supposed to do here? It sure didn't look like a raffle to me. I was beginning to regret my decision to be part of Pride Night.

Suddenly a little old lady bounced into the room. "Where are the helpers?" she demanded, looking around. "You have less than thirty minutes to set this up. People will be here to buy tickets. And where's the guitar?"

I shrugged my shoulders. She harrumphed and left, telling me to "get moving." I immediately started texting Kiki, Marcy, and Luzie:

me: Yo! Need help! PLEEZ!

I didn't wait for their replies and struggled to take down some chairs and set them up. Just then three well-dressed, great-looking guys showed up. One was carrying a guitar and a stand to put it on, another had a roll of raffle tickets and a box, and the third carried a folding table.

"Hi. Where do you want this?" the one with the guitar asked.

"Just set it up in front, so people can see it. And you two, help with the chairs. I'm really glad you guys showed up."

The guys looked at each other and smiled. Then they pitched in and chairs started to line up in tidy rows. I set up the folding table next to the guitar and arranged the tickets and the raffle box.

Okay, now it was coming together. That wasn't so bad. Then the guy who brought the guitar whipped out a black permanent marker and started writing on the guitar! I freaked and grabbed it out of his hand, "Are you crazy?" I yelled. "We're supposed to raffle this off. You're gonna ruin it!"

Just as I was mid-rant, waving the marker in the air like an idiot, Marcy burst into the room followed closely by Kiki and Luzie.

Marcy called out, "Here we..." She stopped dead in her tracks, and Luzie and Kiki bumped into her like a circus-clown routine.

I ♡ The Jonas Brothers

"Omigod," I heard Kiki mutter as they stood there with their mouths open.

"What?" I said. My three helpers were cracking up.

"Harlee, why are you yelling at the Jonas Brothers?" Marcy asked.

"Don't be silly, these guys are the help... ers..." I stopped and looked them over, pointing the marker at each one, "Joe...Nick...Kevin." *Oh, no! What have I done?*

I put my hand over my mouth and backed up. I wished I could just hide. Those girls were right: some celebrity reporter! *I hadn't even recognized them!*

"I'm so sorry," I stammered. "I was in such a hurry..."

"Hey, no problem. We were glad to help, weren't we guys?" Kevin said.

Joe and Nick laughed and nodded in agreement. "It's nice *not* to be recognized sometimes," Joe said. "Yeah, it's like being normal for a while," Nick added.

By now, Luzie, Marcy, and Kiki had recovered from their shock and came up to meet the Jonas boys. Handshakes and smiles all around made the moment fun. I handed the marker back to Kevin.

"I think you were all going to sign the guitar."

"Right. Let's do it," Kevin replied.

As the Jonas Brothers signed the guitar, Luzie and I finished up the chairs, artistic Marcy made a sign for the guitar and a tickets-for-sale sign, while Kiki ran to the office to get a cash box.

Joe finished signing and said, "We'd better get going before people start coming in."

Kiki joined in, "Yeah, we have to go too. We have dates for a dance at our high school, and we're going to be late if we don't leave like right now."

My BFFs said good-bye to the Jonas brothers and hurried off, chatting excitedly. The

I ♡ The Jonas Brothers

Jonas brothers turned to go, when Nick stopped and asked, "How come you're not going to the dance, Harlee?"

"Oh...it's a long story. But in a nutshell... another girl asked my crush to go, so I decided to do this instead."

"We're just hanging tonight. Why don't we come back and pick you up later. We can drop in on your dance," Kevin offered.

"No...thanks, though. You guys have done enough."

"We'll be here at nine. Be ready. And sell lots of tickets!" Joe said.

After the raffle...

I had just finished cleaning up when the little old lady returned to get the cash box. It was filled to the brim. I sold over two hundred tickets! The little old lady informed me the money would be used to help build playgrounds at inner-city schools. How cool was that?

Just as she was leaving, in popped the Jonas brothers. She waved them off in disgust, saying, "You're late again. It's all cleaned up."

We all burst out laughing. Clearly she didn't have a clue either.

"Are you ready?" Nick asked.

"Sure. My parents said it was okay, but I have to be home by eleven."

"Okay. Let's go," Kevin said as he ushered me out the door.

The drive to the high school was a short one, but I managed to tell the Jonas brothers my whole life history. Then a light bulb went off in my head, and I told them I was going to do my column, "HarteBeat," for the *Hollywodland Star* on them next week. And, if they had no objections, I would like to know some of their faves. That led to a spirited discussion ranging from food to girls and everything in between. *This was the scoop of the century!*

I ♡ The Jonas Brothers

I was so stoked. The column on the Jonas Brothers would be great with all the personal details, and I could still meet the deadline if my friends helped with some research. I happily jotted down everything they said, trying to keep it all organized.

When we finally pulled into the parking lot, I had pages of notes! I thanked them all for being so open as we walked to the gym. "That was a fun interview," Joe said. "Yeah, it was like a conversation with a friend," Nick added.

I felt so good, but little did I know the best was yet to come.

When the four of us walked into the dance, no one seemed to take any notice. It was dark, and the colored lights were focused on the dance floor where Kiki and Toby were taking center stage. *I didn't know Toby could dance....* Finally I spotted Marcy and Zack talking to Luzie and Joey, and with the Jonas brothers tagging along, I headed over. Big mistake!

The little blonde freshman with braces started squealing, "The Jonas Brothers! Omigod!" Everyone looked to where she was pointing. The Jonas brothers jumped up on the stage, and Kevin took the mic. The place was a madhouse!

"Hey, everybody! Harlee invited us here tonight to say hello to all of you," Kevin said. "Harlee's a very special person, and we're happy we got to meet her."

Someone started clapping. I looked over and saw that it was Toby and Kiki. All the kids joined in, except for Sondra, who did not look too happy. They were clapping for me, and it felt great.

Then Joe took the mic, "How about a song? If the band doesn't mind, we'll sing 'When You Look Me in the Eyes,' but for this dance, the boys need to ask the girls."

The crowd responded with cheers, and by the time the first notes were played, everyone had partnered up on the dance floor.

I ♥ The Jonas Brothers

I was taken by the moment and did not realize that Jack was standing next to me.

"Would you like to dance?" he asked.

It took me a moment to catch my breath.

"Yes. I'd love to," I whispered, and we held hands as we made our way to the floor.

It was our first dance, and I felt like I was in a dream. I didn't know what tomorrow would bring for Jack and me, and I didn't care—this was the moment, and it was the best night of my life.

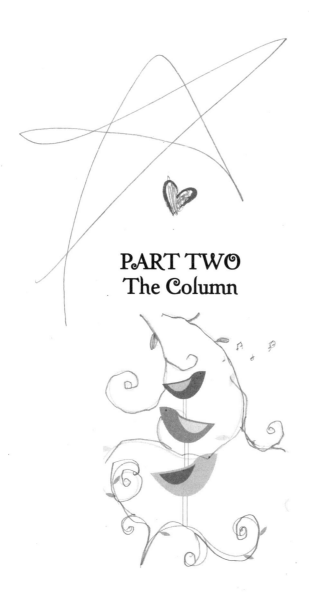

PART TWO
The Column

THE HOLLYWOODLAND STAR
VOL. 11 ISSUE 8 — HOLLYWOOD, CA

NICK

Birthday:
Sept. 16, 1992

Sign: Virgo

Qualities:
reliable, smart, shy, neat

Love match:
Libra

Starstone:
Sardonyx

Element: Earth

Ruling Planet:
Mercury

Color:
Dark green

HarteBeat
by Harlee Harte

I ♥ the Jonas Brothers.

I'm sure there isn't any student at Hollywoodland High who hasn't heard about the surprise visit the Jonas Brothers made to our Turnabout dance. It was insane!

But maybe some of you don't know that the Jonas Brothers also donated a signed guitar to Tinseltown Elementary's Pride Night that was raffled off for charity by yours truly. The raffle was a huge success and resulted in

I 🎵 The Jonas Brothers

JOE

Birthday:
August 15, 1989

Sign: Leo

Qualities:
creative,
generous,
optimistic,
dramatic

Love Match:
Virgo

Starstone: Ruby

Element: Fire

Ruling planet:
The sun

Color: Gold

a big boost to the little kids' efforts to raise money to fund playground renovation in inner city schools. Way to go, little Stars-to-be!

As you all probably know by now, Nick, Joe, and Kevin Jonas personally showed up to deliver the guitar, and I conscripted them (albeit accidentally!) into helping set up. They were great, and I couldn't have asked for more enthusiastic helpers.

So, this week I'm dedicating my column to everything Jonas! Are you ready to get Jonas-blasted? Read on!

In the beginning...

The Jonas Brothers are from Wyckoff, New Jersey, a suburban

KEVIN

Birthday:
Nov. 5, 1987

Sign: Scorpio

Qualities: resourceful, passionate, self-confident, and motivated

Love Match: Sagittarius

Starstone: Opal

Element: Water

Ruling Planet: Pluto

Color: Dark Red

town close to New York City, where they have lived since 1996. But when they were young, the family moved around a lot because of their dad's work as a minister. They lived briefly in Teaneck, New Jersey, birthplace, on November 5, 1987, of the oldest Jonas, Paul Kevin II, named after his dad, who also just goes by Kevin; Arizona, where Joe (Joseph Adam Jonas) was born on August 15, 1989; and Dallas, Texas where Nick (Nicholas Jerry Jonas) entered the world on September 16, 1992. A fourth son, Franklin Nathaniel (Frankie) was born to Kevin and Denise Jonas on September 28, 2000, and he is often referred to as the "Bonus Jonas."

I ♡ The Jonas Brothers

Check it out! The Jonas Brothers are of Italian, Irish, German, and Cherokee Indian descent. Their last name is of Hebrew origin and means "a dove."

When Kevin and Joe were babies, Kevin Sr. and Denise worked at the Christ for the Nations Bible Institute in Dallas, where Kevin Sr. taught songwriting and recorded Christian music, and where Denise, also a singer and proficient in sign language, worked in the registrar's office. They would often often take Christian musical groups to venues around the area and bring along Kevin and Joe in their van outfitted with a crib and little play area in the back. Joe's first car seat was the strongbox they carried with them that held their hard-earned money!

In 1996, the family, now including four-year-old Nick, settled down in New Jersey, when Kevin Sr. accepted the job of pastor at the Assembly of God church in Wyckoff. Family life was simple and fun for the Jonas brothers. It revolved around their dad's church where they would attend the service on Sunday to hear his sermon and listen to him play songs on his guitar. As they got older they would join him in singing to the congregation, and some of the songs they sang were actually written by their dad.

The boys were always surrounded by music at home as well since Kevin Sr. was a pop music buff and introduced them to Carole King and James Taylor songs when they were growing up. Kevin Sr. admired the powerful producers behind hit songs and analyzed the *Billboard* charts on a weekly basis. It was clear he was passionate about music and passed that on to his sons.

Soon Nick's interest in music, and perfect pitch, were apparent to everyone in the family. He would belt out songs using a turkey baster as a pretend microphone and loved putting on musical plays with his brothers and friends in the family's basement for anyone willing to come. Often the kids would sing and dance to the popular tunes of 'N Sync and the Backstreet Boys. Nick never showed much interest in toys, much preferring to make music and sing—and he sought perfection in everything he did. Joe and Kevin were not musical slouches either with Kevin teaching himself to play guitar, and Joe developing an interest in opera.

What were the Jonas Brothers like as little kids?

Kevin was talkative and out going; a high-energy type who often would be hard to shut up. He was friendly and charming to everyone he met.

Joe was the total opposite, quiet and mellow, happily going along. But Joe surprised everyone when he developed a great sense of humor in elementary school and began to use it. He is always ready to make people laugh.

Nick was Mr. Serious, always thinking with an intensity that was surprising in a child. He was very creative and self-directed. Nick strove for perfection in anything he attempted as a child and always followed the rules.

It wasn't long before the boys' early exposure to music led to their talents being put before the public. It began with six-year-old Nick. He loved to go to the beauty salon with his mom when he was a little boy and sing to anyone who would listen for candy money. One day another patron, whose young son had been in *Les Miserables*, suggested to Denise that she seek a manager for little Nick so he could try to land some singing parts. Before long Nick was singing his heart out in such productions as *Annie Get Your Gun* (as Little Jake), *Beauty and the Beast* (as Chip), *A Christmas Carol* (as Tiny Tim), *Les Miserables* (as Gavroche), and, following that, a run as Kurt in *The Sound of Music*. Nick adjusted to his routine well, even though he had to skip school for Wednesday matinees. Pretty soon, older brothers Joe and Kevin started working in the biz, with Joe singing in *Oliver!* and *La Bohème* and Kevin landing commercial work for diverse companies such as Clorox and Burger King.

I 💜 The Jonas Brothers

In 2002, while Nick was in *Beauty and the Beast*, he co-wrote a song with his father called "Joy to the World (A Christmas Prayer)." Nick went on to record this song on an AIDS benefit Christmas album. Nick's single was picked up off the album by INO Records and eventually made it to Christian radio stations...and to the charts. In 2004, Columbia Records became interested in Nick and also signed him. They released his single, "Dear God," followed by a new recording of "Joy to the World (A Christmas Prayer)." Next, Columbia Records planned an album for Nick called *Nicholas Jonas*, containing primarily spiritual songs. Although it was supposed to be released in December 2004, the album was pushed back and saw only limited release. All three brothers had collaborated and written several songs for the album.

When Nick's solo career did not look like it was panning out, Kevin, Joe, and Nick began writing and playing songs together. In early 2005, the new president of Columbia Records, Steve Greenberg, listened to Nick's solo album. He liked Nick's voice but wasn't crazy about the album. However, he was interested enough to listen to the three brothers sing a song they had written called "Please Be Mine." After that performance, the Jonas brothers were signed to Columbia as a group act, known as The Jonas Brothers. Kevin, Joe, and Nick thought long and hard to choose a name that would best identify them, and their alternate name, "Sons of Jonas," came in a close second.

Then the trio was given the opportunity to record their first album for Columbia Records. The Jonas brothers worked hard on *It's About Time*, their debut album for Columbia, working with several well-known songwriters to enhance the songs and quality. But the album, due to be released in February 2006, began to have setbacks, and the release date was pushed back several times during the early part of the year. Much of the trouble was caused by a turnaround in the executive leadership of Sony, of which Columbia Records was

I ♡ The Jonas Brothers

a part. The new executives were looking for another lead single to put on the album. The Jonas Brothers band had already released their first single in December 2005, "Mandy," which did quite well as a music video. The song was featured in Nickelodeon's made-for-television movie, *Zoey 101: Spring Break-Up*. The Jonas Brothers went on during the year to both cover and write several songs and found their music being featured on Cartoon Network and MTV, among others.

To promote the unknown group and their upcoming album, Columbia wanted to get their music and their faces before the public to build a fan base. So all of a sudden they were opening for big acts like Kelly Clarkson, the Backstreet Boys, Jesse McCartney, and others, and performing gigs all over the map. They spent much of the last half of 2005 touring with Aly & AJ and The Cheetah Girls on an anti-drug tour. Soon, all three boys were missing tons of school at Eastern Christian and would eventually have to be home schooled.

One day during this grueling period, Joe noticed that his little brother Nick had lost a lot of weight. He was practically skin and bones. Denise and Kevin rushed Nick to the hospital where he was diagnosed with diabetes. The whole family rallied around Nick with Denise keeping a constant vigil at his bedside. No one knew if the Jonas Brothers band would be able to go on. But with information and counseling the family learned that diabetes could be effectively managed. As 13-year-old Nick told *Rolling Stone* magazine, "After about the second day in the hospital, I realized it'd be all right. It would just take time and understanding to manage it."

Diabetes is is one of the most prevalent chronic diseases among children in the United States, affecting about 150,000 children under the age of eighteen. Diabetes occurs when the body does not produce enough insulin—a hormone that converts sugar, starches, and other food into energy necessary for life.

I ♥ The Jonas Brothers

Now Nick wears an insulin pump on his back that keeps his insulin level stable, and he checks his status all day long by pricking his finger to see if he needs to eat something to correct his blood-sugar levels. Although it took about nine months for Nick to get the routine down and feel normal again, there are times when things just don't work out, and he has to give himself a shot.

Check it out!

Type 1, or juvenile diabetes, happens most often in children and young adults but can appear at any age.

Symptoms may include:
- Being very thirsty
- Urinating often
- Feeling very hungry or tired
- Losing weight without trying
- Having sores that heal slowly
- Having dry, itchy skin
- Losing the feeling in your feet or having tingling in your feet
- Having blurry eyesight

source: National Library of Medicine/National Institutes of Health

The Jonas Brothers' bodyguard, Big Rob, always carries a syringe of insulin to be ready for any emergency. Because of his heavy schedule and touring, Nick is also monitored closely by his family to help keep the diabetes under control.

In 2008, Nick Jonas became a spokesman for Bayer Diabetes Care. He helps encourage children to properly manage their diabetes with his presence on Bayer's special Web site: www.NicksSimpleWins.com. On this site, kids with diabetes and their family members can log on to find out more about how Nick deals with diabetes and share his experiences through a blog. The Web site encourages a positive outlook and positive experiences, called Simple Wins, for kids dealing with and managing diabetes. In response to his need to express himself about his struggle with diabetes, Nick wrote the highly personal lyrics to the song "A Little Bit Longer" while the three brothers were recording their third album.

I 💜 The Jonas Brothers

The Jonas Brothers started their own charitable organization, Change for the Children, and Nick's D-Division is his part of the organization devoted to supporting people with diabetes, raising money for research, and building public awareness. Nick says on the Web site, "Nearly every day I hear from someone like me who says that I made them feel it's OK to have diabetes and that's really cool that I can do that!" Way to go, Nick!

The Change for the Children Foundation is Kevin, Joe, and Nick's way of giving back to the community by supporting programs that not only motivate and inspire children facing adversity in their lives but also offer those kids a chance to develop confidence and determination to succeed. The brothers believe strongly that the best way to help kids is through active participation by their peers, so their organization provides opportunities for kids to help those less fortunate than themselves. To help their foundation achieve its goals, the Jonas brothers donate 10% of their earnings for its use. Change for the Children supports five charities and calls upon young people to donate and volunteer. Take a look at www.changeforthechildren.org and check out the Volunteer Text Program. It's a really cool way to get involved!

Down and up...

It's About Time lived up to its name when it finally came out in August 2006, a full six months after its intended release. But, unfortunately, it saw only a limited release of 50,000 copies. Because of its lack of availability, the album is considered a collectible today with albums selling on eBay for $200-$300. So if you have a copy, hang on to it...it could be even more valuable someday! Columbia Records dropped The Jonas Brothers early in 2007. The boys were disappointed as they had devoted

I 💜 The Jonas Brothers

themselves to the exhausting touring schedule set by Columbia and had fulfilled all their obligations.

But they weren't idle for long.

While the brothers were busy singing the jingle in commercials for Baby Bottle Pops, the musical wheels were turning in the boardroom. Bob Cavallo, chairman of Buena Vista Music Group, had been preparing to pounce on the Jonas boys from the time he first heard about the Columbia Records split. Cavallo, who was a seasoned manager of such groups as the Lovin' Spoonful, Earth, Wind and Fire, and Prince, had been watching the band and was impressed by their musical ability.

Cavallo brought the boys to Disney, and before long they had their first album under the Hollywood Records label, *Jonas Brothers*, which went on to sell 1.4 million copies after its release in August 2007. The album climbed to No. 5 on the *Billboard* Hot 200 chart in the first week. Two successful singles and music videos spun off this album, "Hold On" and "S.O.S." And the *Jonas Brothers* album had been recorded in only 21 days!

The Jonas Brothers owe a lot to Disney. It was opening for Disney-diva Miley Cyrus that put them squarely on the radar of millions of teen consumers and gave them a built-in, ready-made audience. But the boys are quick to point out that they are not Disney-character creations—they play their own instruments, write their own songs, and are really brothers. They even had their acting debut on *Hannah Montana*, in an episode titled "Me and Mr. Jonas and Mr. Jonas and Mr. Jonas."

More and more the Jonas Brothers were showing up on the little screen: they sang two songs at the Miss Teen USA pageant; performed at the closing ceremonies of the Disney Channel Games; were presenters (along with Miley) at the Teen Choice Awards; performed "S.O.S" at the American Music Awards; made an appearance at Macy's

I ♡ The Jonas Brothers

annual Thanksgiving Day Parade; and rounded out the year by singing two songs in New York for *Dick Clark's New Year's Rockin' Eve.*

Between all this, the brothers were invited to the White House twice: once for the annual Easter Egg Roll where they sang the National Anthem, and another time when they performed several songs at the Celebrating Women in Sports event. Those must have been exciting times for the kids from New Jersey!

In January 2008, the brothers embarked on their Look Me in the Eyes tour, which featured some songs from their upcoming third album, *A Little Bit Longer.* Then The Jonas Brothers headed off to open up for Avril Lavigne's Best Damn Tour on the European segment. By opening for Avril, it was hoped that the band would find another audience and further expand its fan base.

While on their Look Me in the Eyes tour, the Jonas gang participated in a Disney Channel reality series called, *Jonas Brothers: Living the Dream.*

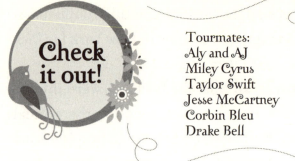

Check it out!

Tourmates:
Aly and AJ
Miley Cyrus
Taylor Swift
Jesse McCartney
Corbin Bleu
Drake Bell

Premiering in May 2008, the show documented the lives of the brothers while on tour and featured clips of rehearsals, traveling, performing, and even studying. The show, which ended in September, gave an intimate glance of the Jonas brothers' personal lives with their family and friends, at work and at play.

Also in 2008, the boys were the stars of Disney Channel's original movie, *Camp Rock*, along with Demi Lovato. This was a great acting experience for the trio as they were the featured players, especially Joe who played the lead. The movie centered on a musically talented girl from a working class family, Mitchie Torres, played by Demi Lovato, whose dream was to attend Camp Rock, a prestigious music camp that helped young musicians hone their skills and bring them to a professional level. However, Mitchie's family could not afford the tuition to send her. But her mom came to the rescue by getting a job at the camp as a cook, so the tuition was discounted, and Mitchie was able to go.

Mitchie was so excited, but when she arrived at Camp Rock she was intimidated by the wealth and privilege around her. She soon was befriended by Caitlyn (Alyson Stoner), but Mitchie felt she needed to impress the popular girls (led by Tess) and told everyone her mom was a powerful music producer. This got her in the clique, and she even sang backup for the snooty girls.

In the meantime, popular teen band Connect 3 had just had their summer tour canceled, and the lead singer, Shane Gray (Joe Jonas), seemed to be disinterested in music and the band. In an effort to jumpstart Shane, his fellow bandmates, Jason (Kevin Jonas) and Nate (Nick Jonas), thought that a stint in Camp Rock would be a good idea. Shane and Mitchie became friends almost immediately as Shane was drawn to Mitchie's wonderful voice, and Mitchie treated Shane like a real friend instead of a star and appreciated his musical creativity.

Tess became jealous of Mitchie's and Shane's friendship and found out the truth about Mitchie's mother. The catty, mean girl went on a vendetta to make sure Mitchie and Caitlyn did not get to perform at the Final Jam, the camp's ending competition. But Mitchie prevailed and had to perform in front of a panel of judges, including Shane, Nate, and Jason. And she triumphed!

The Jonas Brothers got along with everyone on the set, making good friends and learning a lot about the process of making a movie and acting. Alyson Stoner had a very positive experience with them and described her feelings about each Jonas when she told MTV News: "I'd say Nick is very passionate and focused and driven.... Joe is a free spirit, but he's also very supportive when you need him there as a friend and brother. And Kevin is so gentlemanly and so respectful of everyone's privacy, or when they need something to happen, he gets right on it. And I admire them and respect them so much."

While they were making the movie, Kevin, Joe, and Nick lent their talents to Demi Lovato's album, *Don't Forget*, co-writing and producing several songs. After they finished making *Camp Rock*, the movie soundtrack was released and made it to #3 on the *Billboard* charts. While all this was happening, *Camp Rock 2* was already in the works, and the Jonas brothers were ready to join the cast again for the proposed 2010 release. And the acting bug must have really taken hold because in October 2008 it was announced that the Jonas brothers will be making their first feature film, *Walter the Farting Dog*, which is an adaptation of the best-selling books by William Kotzwinkle and Glenn Murray. The family-oriented film is planned for release in 2010. As a "bonus" it will also feature the bonus Jonas, young Frankie.

Next up for the talented trio was their Burning Up Tour. This North American tour had a specific purpose to promote their upcoming album *A Little Bit Longer* and promote the soundtrack from *Camp Rock*. Songs from their first two albums, *It's About Time* and *Jonas Brothers* were also featured. This tour showcased two performances in Anaheim, California, with Taylor Swift who sang some singles from her *Taylor Swift* album.

Check it out!

Tour Bus Must-Have Snacks:
Diet Dr Pepper
Dibs ice cream treats
Smucker's Uncrustables PB&J sandwiches

I ♡ The Jonas Brothers

A lot of fun, exciting things bombarded Kevin, Joe, and Nick during 2008. Among them was making history as the youngest band ever to be on the cover of *Rolling Stone* magazine! Another first for the guys was donating the clothes they wore on their album cover to the Rock and Roll Hall of Fame in Cleveland, Ohio, for an exhibit showcasing some of the most popular contemporary artists.

February 2009 ushered in the Disney big-screen, pop-rock concert film, *Jonas Brothers: The 3D Concert Experience*, which gave viewers behind-the-scenes glimpses of the 2008 Jonas Brothers Burning Up tour. *Variety* remarked about the documentary: "The Disney machine is hoping that 'Jonas Brothers' will be a must-see for tween and teen girls. During their recent concert tour, the pop band incited near-mayhem among fans." Despite the hype, though, the movie disappointed at the box office with under $20 million in sales. But it didn't detract from the band's appeal, which was stronger than ever. Sun Media reported that in a teleconference interview with music writers, Joe weighed in on the movie: "We were, in our own hearts, kind of satisfied with whatever [numbers] we got and our fans really showed up—that's what we thought was amazing. I mean, it was cool for us to have the second largest grossing concert film of all time."

An episode of the comic *South Park* in March 2009 dropped some controversy into the laps of the Pied-Piper trio of curly-haired pop stars. Kevin, Joe, and Nick were mercilessly satirized and made fun of in the segment for their clean-living ways and values, and the episode also zoomed in on some of Disney's tween-marketing tactics. The Jonas brothers say they have not watched the controversial episode, but nonetheless their publicist has forbidden reporters from asking the band about it. Despite the gag order, Dose.ca reported that "the boys insist they were cool with it." They quoted Nick as saying, "I think we always like to be open to make fun of ourselves...we'll be the first to."

I 💟 The Jonas Brothers

In fact, they have done just that. On their first appearance on *David Letterman* the brothers read their own top ten list as reported by huffingtonpost.com:

10. Our new 3D concert film puts you right in the middle of a six-hour tour bus ride from Pittsburgh to Albany.

9. Often we are astonished by how adorable we are.

8. Sometimes we lather, rinse, repeat and then repeat again!

7. Last Sunday night, I won a Grammy for "Best New Jonas."

6. Osama said he'd come out of hiding if we'd meet his 15-year-old niece.

5. One time when we were on the road, things got really crazy and we stayed up until 10:30.

4. We've seen Paul Blart: Mall Cop 27 times.

3. Once a week we get mail for Dr. Joyce Brothers.

2. We have no idea who that old dude behind the desk is.

DRUMROLL, PLEASE

1. A couple years back, Angelina Jolie tried to adopt us.

In May 2009, the Jonas Brothers had yet another first: their own TV showed debuted called *JONAS*. In this Disney Channel sitcom, Kevin (21), Joe (19), and Nick (16) play the Lucas brothers, pop stars who are desperately trying to handle their fame and live normal high school lives. The brothers live with their mother Sandy, father Tom, and younger brother Frankie (*yes*...really the Bonus Jonas) in a fire station that has been converted to a house. The band's name comes from Jonas Street where they live. In the storyline, the Lucas boys have known Stella Malone, their personal stylist and friend, since Stella was five years old, and they all attend Horace Mantis Academy together along with Stella's best friend and JONAS' self-proclaimed biggest fan, Macy. Madcap hijinks and slapstick abound when the characters get in and out of trouble and deal with problems on a daily basis. Like real life jacked up a notch or two on the comedic scale!

I ♥ The Jonas Brothers

The Jonas Brothers were psyched to do the show. As Joe told *People*, "We're used to touring and traveling. The show is a fun new thing."

Although the show opened well with four million viewers on its Saturday night premiere opposite *iCarly*, it soon was moved to Sunday night as it failed to draw in the viewers after that. The show had mixed reviews in the media. As the *New York Times* put it, the sitcom "...is a calculated, perhaps fearful step backward, a reclamation of innocence." *Variety* chimed in with, "Those who do not swoon and emit piercing squeals at the sight of Kevin, Joe and Nick Jonas will still find some amiable charm within this slick packaging, even if it's nothing that couldn't be mistaken for 'The Monkees' four decades ago." And the *Los Angeles Times* said, "There's nothing to complain about here, and much to like...they are less manufactured than many young pop sensations—they write almost all their songs.... They're bona fide pop stars still young enough to be playing at being pop stars."

But despite the weak start, Disney had big plans around the show, opting to come out with a Jonas Brothers clothing line based on *JONAS*. But you'll never see the Jonas guys wearing these threads—because they are for girls! Disney figured (and quite accurately!) that boys are not going to buy clothes with handsome heartthrobs on the label, even if they are fashion statements, but girls...that's a totally different story. So the entire line is marketed at tween girls.

The clothing takes it fashion cues from the attire the kids wear at the fictitious private school the characters attend, Horace Mantis Academy. So it's all preppy argyles and plaids, t-shirts, ruffled polos, woven tops, leggings, skirts and jeans, some clothes even sporting the school's logo. Time will tell whether or not the line will be a hit, but Wal-Mart, KMart, and J.C.Penney are all stocking the line.

Amidst all this activity, the Jonas boys were set to release a new album scheduled for June 2009. The album, *Lines, Vines and Trying Times*, was

I ♥ The Jonas Brothers

their fourth, and its title sparked curiosity about its meaning. Nick Jonas explained the title to *Rolling Stone* magazine as "a bit of poetry we came up with on the set for the TV show." He went on to say, "Lines are something that someone feeds you, whether it's good or bad. Vines are the things that get in the way of the path that you're on, and trying times...we're aware of what's going on in the world and we're trying to bring some light to it." The brothers drew inspiration from their own experiences to write the album's songs and also tried their hands at using more metaphors in the lyrics. This time they experimented with different musical instruments and were influenced musically by Elvis Costello, The Zutons, Coldplay, and Neil Diamond. The result was a really cool album that showcased their many talents!

The first single from the album, "Paranoid," created swirling rumors that the song was actually Joe's musical retort to his old crush Taylor Swift's sad song "Forever and Always" from her 2008

Fearless album about her very publicized breakup with him. Taylor even filmed a video for her MySpace where she is holding a Joe Jonas doll and talks about their split saying, "This one even comes with a phone so it can break up with other dolls!" Many fans thought Joe was attacking her in retaliation for her lyrics in which she muses if she said *something way too honest* that forced him to *run and hide like a scared little boy*. The lyrics in the edgy "Paranoid" seem to many to be Joe's reply: *That's why my ex is still my ex/I never trust a word she says/I'm running all the background checks/And she's freaking out*. Kevin, Joe, and Nick denied the rumors, with Nick quoted on disneydreaming.com, "This is really funny because people think this is about something particular but the truth to that is it's one of the only songs of the record that's not about a direct personal experience." Whatever! Got an opinion? Write a comment on my Facebook wall!

I ♡ The Jonas Brothers

To promote the album, the Jonas Brothers embarked on an ambitious world tour that took them throughout North America, South America, and Europe. In a new twist for this tour, the band used a 144-foot stage (as opposed to the usual 35-45 feet) to put themselves smack dab in the middle of their screaming fans and allow them to get an upfront and personal view. It was a show in-the-round concept that also featured a huge circular water screen, special laser video effects and a giant crane extending over the audience. Demi Lovato, Wonder Girls (a popular Asian all-girl group), Jessie James, Honor Society, and Jordin Sparks all performed on the tour at designated venues.

Before the start of the tour in Dallas, Joe said that the tour was all about connecting with the fans and trying to give them a concert they would never forget. And in true Jonas fashion, they delivered exactly what they promised, playing sold-out venues across the globe to hordes of screaming fans!

The Jonas Brothers have released four albums to date:

It's About Time (2006)
Jonas Brothers (2007)
A Little Bit Longer (2008)
Lines, Vines and Trying Times (2009)

Through May 2009, the Jonas Brothers have sold over 8.1 million albums worldwide and have a total of 36 gold and platinum records.

They were nominated for a Grammy in 2008 for Best New Artist but didn't win; however, they did pick up the award for Breakthrough Artist from the American Music Awards. They have won a total of sixteen awards, including five Teen Choice Awards and two Nickelodeon Kids' Choice awards.

What about the guys and their fans? The three brothers share their often-silly homemade videos with their fans and never complain about their meet-and-greets with them. In fact, they actually enjoy them. Kevin, Joe, and Nick appreciate their many fans, and though they are surprised sometimes at the fans' reactions to them in public, they take it all in stride. They like to connect with their fans on different levels through fan-site blogs, MySpace, and YouTube. Lucky for us!

Check it out! At their concerts, the Jonas Brothers often like to pull diehard fans out of the nosebleed seats and put them in the front row.

In an interview with the *LA Times*, the Jonas brothers gave some insight on how they feel about screaming fans, and Nick said, "...you just take a step at a time. But it's fun. We love what we do and we love that our fans are so supportive and so amazing. They're the best."

And ever-the-funny-guy Joe had something to say about frantic fans on *David Letterman*:

"There's a lot of screaming involved," Joe said. "Sometimes you don't know what to do 'cause you think it's 'Cloverfield' coming around the corner and you just hear, 'Rarrrhh!'"

What's with the rings? They have taken some hits for wearing purity rings (often called promise rings) but they each made their own decision to do so when they were ready. To The Jonas Brothers the rings signify respecting themselves as well as others and being true to their values. They don't go around preaching about them or their faith, but they don't try to sweep their spirituality under the rug either. They have found a way to perform in the pop culture word, but remain true to themselves.

What are the Jonas Brothers' interview rules?
An interviewer cannot ask:

I 💟 The Jonas Brothers

1. Questions about any of their girlfriends past, present or suspected.

2. Questions about their religion or purity rings.

3. Questions about the *South Park* episode making fun of the brothers and their purity rings.

Questions about their music and upcoming projects are always welcomed, but they shy away from anything to do with their personal lives, and most often, will either evade the sticky question or give a silly answer to defuse it.

THE JOBROS AND GIRLS

Kevin: Danielle Deleasa and Kevin met in 2007 while vacationing with their families. They became engaged in July 2009.

Joe: Joe reportedly dumped country songstress Taylor Swift for actress Camilla Belle.

Nick: Nick has dated fellow Disney-mates Miley Cyrus (twice!) and Selena Gomez.

Interviewers complain that between the controls placed on the interviews by their publicist, and the Jonas brothers' own reticence to talk about themselves in anything other than superficial terms, that it is difficult to report anything that hasn't been heard a hundred times.

Fans always want to know more...that's what keeps them interested, but there is another side to the coin: stars deserve their privacy.

What do you think? Let me know!

Their look is so cool. Tell me about it. We all know about those skinny jeans, button-downs, and ties, but there's much more individuality in their styles! They definitely have a polished, professional look, but it's not all business—it's got a fun vibe too.

Kevin goes for a cool, well-tailored style that is classier, and loves wearing classics like a leather bomber jacket. He admits he likes more of a Victorian look and likes to dress up with ascots, scarves, and Dior Homme suits. He likes the cut, fabric and slim lines of the suits and is in style heaven when he pairs them with a simple white shirt.

Joe loves to create drama using color in his wardrobe. He'll often throw on a bright shirt or sweater for that extra sizzle and likes sweater-vest combos. Sometimes he'll ditch the color and go all black for a totally hip look. His style is also influenced by the '70s and '80s, and he has a penchant for gold jewelry, colorful socks, hats, and vintage scarves. Levi's Capital E colored matchstick jeans and Superga sneakers in different colors are his faves.

Nick has called his look "formal rock" with his high-top sneakers and jackets paired with white shirts with rolled up sleeves. Although he says J. Lindeberg and Dior are his favorite labels, he does lean toward a preppy look, wearing a lot of Ralph Lauren. He likes cardigans, vintage-style leather jackets, and jeans with a more traditional fit, like A.P.C. and their New Cure slim raw denim.

The guys have also been spotted sporting Phillip Lim T-Shirts, bright colored jeans, Ray-Ban Wayfarers, Brooks Brothers Black Fleece Label, and Chelsea boots.

Where do they live? The Jonas brothers live in Los Angeles now, though they also have a huge home in the Dallas suburbs where they like to go to wind down and relax. They love to play golf and ride their dirt bikes there.

Read the **Spotlights** to find out more personal stuff, fun facts, and insane trivia I dug up on each totally hot bro!

Spotlight on KEVIN

BD: November 5, 1987
Nickname: K2
Height: 5'9"
Weight: 135 lbs.
Hair: Brown, curly
Eyes: Green/Hazel

I 💟 The Jonas Brothers

Paul Kevin Jonas II, or just "Kevin," plays lead guitar in The Jonas Brothers band as well as backup vocals. Kevin taught himself to play guitar when he was twelve years old. He describes himself as being "super-hyper" as a young kid and pretty much of a loner when he was thirteen. He still has a lot of energy, which he pours into his guitar playing onstage and loves to perform before live audiences in concerts. Kevin's favorite songs to perform are "S.O.S" and "Burning Up" and he likes to describe the band's sound as "Music on Red Bull."

In school, Kevin liked Latin and History and was fascinated with the Dark Ages period. He enjoyed the sport of pole vaulting and credits it with helping him make friends. He admits that waking up early was the thing he disliked most about school. Although Kevin graduated from high school after being home schooled after his sophomore year, he has not attended college, opting to fully explore his music career.

Kevin has been linked romantically to Zoe Myers, whom he dated for a while back in 2007, but most recently he hit the gossip columns with Danielle Deleasa whom he met in May 2007 while vacationing with his family in the Bahamas. Early in 2009, rumors were swirling that he had bought her an engagement ring, and a photo of the two of them smooching in Malibu, California, pushed the rumor mill into high gear. Kevin denied the engagement rumor (and subsequent "married" rumor), but did admit that he would like to marry young like his parents did. Then in July 2009, Kevin really did pop the question to Danielle, and the two became officially engaged!

Kevin says that he first notices confidence in a girl and admires girls with strong beliefs. He also admits that he likes girls who are good listeners, as he loves to talk, and girls who are relaxed and comfortable to be with who can make him laugh!

But, as a group, the Jonas brothers like to keep their private lives private, concentrating on

I 🖤 The Jonas Brothers

their music and their fans, and avoiding the missteps that lead to public embarrassment…so oldest brother Kevin will let his fans know about his relationships when he is ready.

Kevin admits to being somewhat of a sugar junkie. He can't stand fruit of any kind, especially bananas. He's more likely to reach for a carton of Rocky Road ice cream and some chocolate cake! On the healthier side, he loves sushi, though a trip to In-N-Out is never out of the question. And Starbucks is definitely a must have!

Quirky Kevin won't sleep in an unmade bed—it has to be made up before he will get in; watches music videos while eating breakfast; and won't wear a shirt more than two times. He gets along with his little brothers, Nick and Joe, but can't take it when they try to boss him around or tell him how to drive. But he readily admits he admires Nick for his focus and music skills, and Joe for his ability to make people laugh.

Harlee Harte

Spotlight on JOE

BD: August 15, 1989
Nickname: JJ or DJ Danger
Height: 5'10"
Weight: 140 lbs.
Hair: Black, straight
Eyes: Brown

Joseph Adam Jonas, or Joe as he is called, performs in a variety of ways with the group. He is a talented musician and wears many hats: he does lead vocals, and percussion, guitar, and keyboard as needed for a particular song. Joe never had the desire to become a singer and thought that he would wind up being a comedian. Joe is known to be the comic of the group, and is quick to laugh and make others laugh. This is a very different personality than he displayed as a young child, when he was often described as "quiet." Joe is also

I ♡ The Jonas Brothers

considered by many fans to be the heartthrob of the three brothers and also the most romantic.

Joe's much-publicized breakup with Taylor Swift and his romance with Camilla Belle sent the gossip mags and celeb Web sites into high gear as they fell over each other to report the latest on Joe's love life. Rumors ranged from Joe and Camilla hunting for their own private love nest to their vacations together and Dodger game dates. It seems like Joe will always be the Jonas brother at the forefront of the love and dating gossip, although he says he didn't have his first kiss until he was sixteen! Joe likes to make the first moves and is not shy about letting a girl know he likes her. He uses compliments, little hugs, and lots of smiles to get a girl's attention.

Joe loves clothes and mixing in color. A little vain, he takes a long time to get ready and always has to ask his brothers how he looks over and over. Joe fusses over his hair, often cited on fan sites as his "most prized possession," and hates bad hair days.

Joe is also known for his YouTube video antics, one of which landed him in the hospital to get about 50 stitches in his head when the stunt went wrong. Despite this, Joe still swears by YouTube and says it is his favorite Web site. Joe also tripped onstage at the American Music Awards and cut his hand on some broken glass, but much to his credit, he just kept on performing without losing a beat. He later made light of the incident saying it was "just a little blood, but whatever, rock and roll." So Joe appears to be not only romantic but accident prone too! That's why he is often called "DJ Danger."

Joe has said that his favorite thing about school was his desk, but also admits that he liked Physics and Social Studies. He is also fascinated with the '60s and '70s but would also like to go to the moon. If he ever goes to college he would probably major in theater arts. Joe, the quiet child, really began to come out of his shell around third grade, much to everyone's surprise, by displaying a really

I ♡ The Jonas Brothers

good sense of humor. He remembers one incident at school when he was sent to the principal's office on the very first day for playing a prank on his friends. He has since learned to keep his comedic side in check. But it must be hard for him, because he says that everything makes him laugh!

For all of you who think he is just perfect, Joe does have some down side. He just can't seem to get out of bed in the morning for one, and he is considered to be the loudest, messiest (although Kevin gets that nod too) and the laziest of the three brothers. And he bites his nails.

Where does Joe think he'll be in five years? He answered that question for *Seventeen* magazine: "I guess personally, I would love to do more acting, maybe movies—that would be really cool.... And maybe write a book one day, because I love to read."

Harlee Harte

Spotlight on Nick:

BD: September 16, 1992
Nickname:
Mr. President or Nick J.
Height: 5'8"
Weight: 130 lbs.
Hair: Brown, curly
Eyes: Brown

Nicholas Jerry Jonas, who goes by Nick, is an integral part of the Jonas Brothers band. He performs lead vocals, plays rhythm guitar and piano, and occasionally drums. Nick, although he is the youngest, is the band's leader and chief song architect. Many fans and critics consider Nick to be the most musically talented of the group with the best voice. Songwriting is an outlet for serious-minded, sensitive Nick—it gives him a way to express his feelings.

I ♡ The Jonas Brothers

But what would ultra-talented Nick do if he couldn't be a musician? The answer is surprising: He would be a professional athlete in either baseball or golf. Nick is really into both sports and loves playing golf when he's home in Dallas and zipping around the green in his golf cart, but he is also a huge Yankees and Derek Jeter fan. He also enjoys watching pro-football, especially the NY Giants.

Nick has not been linked to too many girls in the press with the exception of a brief stint with Selena Gomez and a young crush on Miley Cyrus. Miley and Nick had something going when he was fourteen that lasted a few months before it fell apart. That past relationship took an interesting twist when it became new again as the two older, wiser celebs began seeing each other again in mid-2009. Though Nick has said he isn't big on public displays of affection, it may be difficult to keep his private moments private with the ever-watchful paparazzi waiting to capture a kiss or even a hand-holding on film.

What does Nick like in a girl? He may be on the quiet side, but he's had no problem coming up with answers to that question. Nick likes girlie-girls who act like ladies and like to wear dresses, and he doesn't like it when girls come on too strong. He likes a girl who is confident and independent, as he feels he doesn't have to entertain her all the time. Nick is sometimes oblivious to flirting and can't tell whether a girl likes him or not. He would never date a girl with a bad attitude, and he definitely needs a girl who would understand his crazy schedule. He admits that he gets nervous when he calls a girl, so he texts instead but says it's just because he is quiet, not shy. So being a quiet girl is a plus for him too. All in all, Nick likes girls who make him feel happy and make him smile.

Nick graduated from high school in June 2009. Being home-schooled, there was no actual cap and gown ceremony, but Nick was very happy to be a member of the Class of 2009. On Twitter he announced his graduation, saying, "I'm happy to

I ♡ The Jonas Brothers

announce I have graduated! Class of '09! Congrats to everyone else who has also graduated this year!" In school, Nick was not a fan of math, opting for spelling and geology as his favorite subjects. Nick admits he is a perfectionist in everything he does. He even keeps his closet neat and tidy! This trait sometimes puts undo pressure on Nick and everyone around him, but he is working on ways to overcome the need to be perfect all the time and to loosen up.

Nick admits to a host of special secret talents such as juggling, the ability to do one-handed cartwheels, and break-dancing. A secret desire of his is to work in *Cirque du Soleil*, so his special talents may find a home someday!

About Jonas Brothers' songs...

The Jonas Brothers write or co-write most of their own songs. Like many artists, they draw upon personal experiences for the lyrics. So the songs reflect teenage life and relationships, though they have inherent universal themes. Love gained and lost, requited and unrequited. Relationships, good or bad, hard or easy. It's all there! Here are some examples:

1. "Lovebug" was written while on the road with friend Miley Cyrus during the Christmas break of the Hannah Montana Tour. The JoBros wrote the song in about 20 minutes in their hotel room. They say that the inspiration for the song came from a variety of ways, but definitely the movie *Juno* played a part. The song is about love that may or may not last, but there will always be a chance to get bitten by the "lovebug again." The "Lovebug" video was inspired by the love story in the movie *The Notebook* and has a 1940s tone.

2. "Mandy" was written about friend of the Jonas family. The boys' mom taught Mandy to sign so she could help hearing-impaired people. Mandy is also Joe's former girlfriend, and she is still a close

I ♡ The Jonas Brothers

friend of the family today. It was the Jonas Brothers first single.

3. "S.O.S." is a song the band enjoys performing. The song, about relationship problems with girlfriends, was written, purportedly, in ten minutes by Nick and was based on a true story. What that true story is, we may never know as the don't-kiss-and-tell Nick will never spill the beans.

4. "Paranoid" is a song many fans think is Joe Jonas' retort to Taylor Swift's "Forever and Always" which was supposedly about her breakup with Joe. There was quite a debate about it when the song came out, but the band denies the rumor, saying that it actually was not based on anything in real life.

5. "Burnin Up" was inspired by the artistry of the musician Prince. Nick has explained that the song is about the instant connection that can happen between two people, like when you meet someone at a party and just click.

6. "Tonight" is about arguments that people get into that cannot be solved in one night. Nick claims it is one of his favorite songs from the *A Little Bit Longer* album. Arguments and disagreements seem to be a recurrent theme with the Jonas guys!

7. "Time for Me to Fly" was an early song written when Nick was only eleven. Many fans mistakenly believe that this song was written after Nick was diagnosed with juvenile diabetes in 2005; however, the song was written for his never-released solo album before then, so it is not about his diabetes. Nick says that he wrote "A Little Bit Longer" in response to his diabetes.

8. "Poison Ivy" is a song that is about an itch that just won't go away, and try as one might, it just keeps on bothering and eating away at you...and you can't resist scratching it. It was rumored that the song was written about the Jonas brothers' ex-girlfriends but they deny that, saying, it is just a

song about the urge some people have to go back to someone that wasn't good for them.

9. "World War III" is easily related to. Everyone has been in a position where someone is picking a fight or fighting with you, and you do not have a clue why. It is about one-sided confrontational relationships with girls from a guy's point of view, of course! This song has not been linked to any particular incident.

10. "Much Better" is a song the Jonas brothers wrote to thank their legions of fans for their continued support. But that's the official line. A lot of fans see it another way, saying the song is about how Joe broke up with Taylor Swift and started dating Camilla Belle and that the song even references Taylor's song "Teardrops on My Guitar." It seems like "Much Better" is open for interpretation!

All in all, the Jonas Brothers are one insanely talented bunch of brothers who will most undoubtedly have a brilliant future in the music business. They set themselves apart from other boy bands by their musicianship and songwriting skills, and their millions of loyal fans will be there for them for a long time to come.

And to those two girls who dissed me in the lunchroom for my lack of JoBros knowledge, I invite you to a JoBros Trivia Challenge. Just name the time and place!

PART THREE
Games and Quizzes

JoBros Trivia Quiz

Are you suffering from OJD? Take the quiz and find out!

1. What did the Jonas Brothers name their first tour van?
   a. Big Bertha
   b. Big Red
   c. Red Robin
   d. Bertha Jonas

2. Which pop princess did the Jonas Brothers' body guard, Big Rob, and personal assistant, Felicia Culotta, used to work for?
   a. Christina Aguilera
   b. Mandy Moore
   c. Britney Spears
   d. The Spice Girls

I ♡ The Jonas Brothers

3. For which music idol do the Jonas Brothers want to create a tribute album?
   a. The Beatles
   b. Johnny Cash
   c. Elvis Costello
   d. The Rolling Stones

4. What is one of the Jonas Brothers' favorite family meals?
   a. Meatloaf
   b. Chicken
   c. Mac 'n cheese
   d. Sweet potato casserole

5. Which Jonas Brothers share a room?
   a. Kevin and Joe
   b. Joe and Nick
   c. Nick and Kevin
   d. They all have their own rooms

6. What do the Jonas Brothers like to do while on breaks in the studio?
   a. Play basketball
   b. Watch movies
   c. Play chess
   d. Prank-call people

7. What movie inspired the song "Lovebug"?
   a. *The Hannah Montana Movie*
   b. *Juno*
   c. *Nick and Norah's Infinite Playlist*
   d. *About a Boy*

8. For which commercial did the Jonas Brothers sing the jingle?
   a. Baby Bottle Pops
   b. Ring Pops
   c. Fruit Roll-ups
   d. Gushers

I ♡ The Jonas Brothers

9. Which of the following is NOT one of the Jonas Brothers' favorite brands?
   a. Ed Hardy
   b. H & M
   c. Vans
   d. Affliction

10. What is the Jonas Brothers' favorite flavor of gum?
    a. Cinnamon
    b. Bubblegum
    c. Spearmint
    d. Fruity

11. Which of the following is NOT one of the Jonas Brothers' favorite boardgames?
    a. Monopoly
    b. Chutes and Ladders
    c. Clue
    d. Operation

12. What is the Jonas Brothers' favorite type of cheese?
   a. Pepper Jack
   b. Swiss
   c. Cheddar
   d. American

13. Where did the first Jonas Brothers song come from?
   a. Their dad wrote it
   b. Nick's journal
   c. A dream that Joe had
   d. A poem Kevin wrote

14. What does the last name "Jonas" mean in its Hebrew origin?
   a. Musical
   b. Dove
   c. Peace
   d. Brother

I ♡ The Jonas Brothers

15. How does Kevin describe the Jonas Brothers'
    music?
    a. "Bubblegum pop"
    b. "Happy catchy pop rock"
    c. "Music on Red Bull"
    d. "Music a race car driver would listen to"

16. How long did it take the Jonas Brothers to
    record their first album?
    a. Two weeks
    b. Three weeks
    c. A month
    d. Two months

17. What is the best advice anyone has given the
    Jonas Brothers?
    a. "Don't talk about your personal life to the media."
    b. "Write from the heart."
    c. "Be careful not to get too caught up in stardom."
    d. "Live like you're at the bottom, even if you're
       at the top."

18. Which pop star have the Jonas Brothers NOT toured with?
   a. Miley Cyrus
   b. Avril Lavigne
   c. Ashley Tisdale
   d. Taylor Swift

19. What are the names of the Jonas Brothers' parents?
   a. Denise and Paul
   b. Deborah and Kevin
   c. Darla and Peter
   d. Darby and Jonathan

20. What do the Jonas Brothers call their youngest brother?
   a. Swanky Franky
   b. The Bonus Jonas
   c. Franky J
   d. Jonas Plus

I ♡ The Jonas Brothers

21. Where was Nick Jonas discovered?
    a. School talent show
    b. Karaoke contest
    c. A hair salon
    d. The mall

22. What were the Jonas Brothers originally going to call themselves?
    a. Sons of Jonas
    b. Team Jonas
    c. The JoBros
    d. The Jonas Brothers Band

23. What videogame do the Jonas Brothers play most often?
    a. Grand Theft Auto
    b. Madden
    c. Kingdom Hearts
    d. Halo

24. What device can Joe not live without?

　　a. iPod

　　b. Laptop

　　c. Camera

　　d. Toaster

25. How does Nick like to eat his hamburgers?

　　a. In a circle, leaving the center for last

　　b. Left to right, like a typewriter

　　c. Upside-down

　　d. Cut up with a fork and knife

26. What was the first CD that Joe owned?

　　a. Hansen

　　b. 'N Sync

　　c. Britney Spears

　　d. The Spice Girls

I 🖤 The Jonas Brothers

27. What does Kevin hate the smell of?

    a. Gasoline

    b. Bananas

    c. Coffee

    d. Grass

28. What was Kevin's first job?

    a. Mowing lawns

    b. Delivering newspapers

    c. Babysitting

    d. Working at a coffee shop

29. What drink does Nick like?

    a. Starbucks Green Tea Frappucinos

    b. Sugar-free Red Bull

    c. Diet Coke

    d. All of the above

30. What school subject do the Jonas Brothers all love?
    a. Social Studies
    b. Science
    c. Spanish
    d. P.E.

I ♥ The Jonas Brothers

Kevin's Faves Word Search

GREEN
COFFEE
RACHEL MCADAMS
VIDEOS
JACK AND BOBBY
BOWLING
FIFTEEN
MONOPOLY
NIKE

IN N OUT
JAMES DEAN
SKATEBOARD
ABOUT A BOY
BUTTERFINGER
SUSHI
EXCELLENT
JEEP

JOHN MAYER
CHRISTMAS
ROCKY ROAD
MADE BED
POLE VAULTING
DANIELLE
GUITAR
OLD SPICE

Which Jonas Brother are you most compatible with? Take this quiz to find out!

1. Out of your group of friends, you would be considered:
   a. The supportive friend
   b. The comedian
   c. The leader

2. Which flavor of ice cream do you like best?
   a. Rocky Road
   b. Chocolate
   c. Cotton Candy

3. What movie do you like best?
   a. *About a Boy*
   b. *Dumb and Dumber*
   c. *Finding Neverland*

I ♥ The Jonas Brothers

4. What sport do you enjoy most?
   a. Pole Vaulting
   b. Wiffle Ball
   c. Baseball

5. Who do you think is the best actress?
   a. Rachel McAdams
   b. Natalie Portman
   c. Keri Lynn Pratt

6. Who do you think is the best actor?
   a. James Dean
   b. Jim Carrey
   c. Matt Long

7. Which show do you like best?
   a. *Jack and Bobby*
   b. *Boy Meets World*
   c. *Lost*

8. What quality do you like best in a guy?
    a. Romantic, outgoing
    b. Funny, quiet
    c. Sensitive, serious

9. You best enjoy the singing style of:
    a. John Mayer
    b. Elvis Costello
    c. Stevie Wonder

10. What candy bar do you like best?
    a. Butterfinger
    b. Twix
    c. Hershey's chocolate

11. Which car do you prefer?
    a. Jeep
    b. Mercedes
    c. Truck

I ♡ The Jonas Brothers

12. Your personality is:
    a. Sweet
    b. Mellow
    c. Flirty

13. What quality catches your eye in another person?
    a. A good heart
    b. A gorgeous smile
    c. Amazing eyes

14. Which food do you prefer?
    a. Sushi
    b. Chicken Sandwich
    c. Steak

15. When it comes to sleeping, you:
    a. Rise with the sun!
    b. Like to wake up and go to sleep around normal times
    c. Sleep in as late as possible and are a night owl

16. Which activities do you enjoy most?
    a. Bowling and playing instruments
    b. Making movies and working out
    c. Playing baseball and tennis and listening to music

17. What toppings do you like most on your pizza?
    a. Plain cheese
    b. BBQ Chicken
    c. No Preference

18. You would like to date a guy who is a:
    a. Racecar Driver
    b. Zookeeper
    c. Comedian

19. You prefer the color:
    a. Green
    b. Lavender
    c. Blue

I ♡ The Jonas Brothers

20. Who is the cutest Jonas Brother?
    a. Kevin
    b. Joe
    c. Nick

Harlee Harte

Joe's Faves Word Search

L	L	P	R	D	A	L	M	A	A	S	D	D	S	O	B	N	O	I
P	I	N	K	B	E	R	R	Y	G	O	M	L	R	N	L	E	O	N
U	O	G	E	M	R	I	A	A	E	E	A	O	X	S	U	A	B	R
E	E	W	K	I	E	S	T	C	R	R	G	I	R	N	E	C	F	A
M	E	A	E	S	S	O	O	C	E	O	R	N	C	R	S	U	R	D
L	E	J	A	R	R	P	E	O	A	T	U	A	I	D	T	I	S	T
W	S	D	N	A	B	D	A	E	H	N	O	M	C	G	N	S	C	S
U	L	A	D	C	E	A	S	I	N	I	F	T	G	M	G	H	D	U
I	L	E	T	S	N	R	R	A	T	M	T	R	L	T	I	O	R	B
W	O	L	L	A	M	H	S	R	A	M	C	O	H	C	T	J	J	E
L	R	S	Z	A	A	I	A	L	R	A	E	P	K	C	A	L	B	O
M	E	Z	C	O	S	N	O	W	C	O	N	E	S	O	Z	S	G	E
W	I	F	F	L	E	B	A	L	L	O	N	I	P	E	R	O	P	A
P	S	Z	O	E	V	O	A	L	I	C	O	L	S	S	D	O	L	V
T	T	B	S	O	G	C	L	E	U	R	C	A	W	I	H	L	T	R
P	O	N	I	A	O	O	M	T	G	S	R	T	V	Y	I	Y	R	S
E	O	U	N	S	C	A	L	R	S	S	U	A	L	M	E	H	F	D
N	T	M	T	P	R	E	B	M	U	D	D	N	A	B	M	U	D	A
E	N	E	F	S	T	A	R	R	Y	S	O	C	K	S	N	G	T	C

BLUE
POWER BAR
JOGGING
CONNECT FOUR
CHOC MARSHMALLOW
PIZZA
GATORADE
PINKBERRY
LACOSTE

MERCEDES
ONLY HOPE
STARRY SOCKS
NATALIE PORTMAN
SNOW CONES
WIFFLE BALL
TOOTSIE ROLLS
MINT OREOS
DR. SEUSS

CHICKEN CUTLET
HEADBANDS
JIM CARREY
BLACK PEARL
DUMB AND DUMBER
GODIVA
TRIX
CAMILLA

I ♥ The Jonas Brothers

Song Scramble Crossword Puzzle

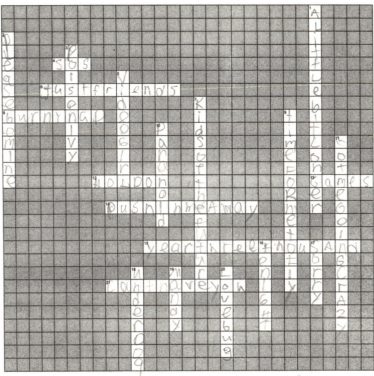

Across
4. SSO
6. SJTU NERDSIF
8. NNIBRU PU
12. LHDO NO
13. MESGA
14. HINPSU EM WYAA
15. RAEY HERET NODSAHUT
21. TACN VAEH OYU

Down
1. A ETILTL ITB ROGNEL
2. APLEES EB NEIM
3. SOPNOI VYI
5. DIVOE LGRI
7. SDIK FO HET UTREFU
9. METI ORF EM OT LYF
10. RIDAPAON
11. OTG EM IGGNO ZARYC
16. GOTIHNT
17. RYORS
18. DGREDONU
19. YNMDA
20. VBOEGUL

Nick's Faves Word Search

- STEAK
- SONGWRITING
- BASEBALL CARDS
- DOG TAGS
- JUNO
- SPRING
- TACO BELL
- STEVIE WONDER
- BLACKBERRY

- GIANTS
- SWITCHFOOT
- APC
- COTTON CANDY
- TENNIS
- BASEBALL
- GOLF
- ELVIS COSTELLO
- SUGAR FREE RED BULL

- BLUE
- MILEY
- MATT LONG
- SPIDERMAN
- LOST
- DIET COKE
- CHEERIOS
- PHILLIP LIM

I ♥ The Jonas Brothers

Answers:

Jo Bros Trivia Quiz

22-30 Correct: You have OJD (Obsessive Jonas Disorder)! You know everything about the boys, even the rarest facts. The entire Jonas family would be proud!

10-22 Correct: You are definitely a Jonas Brothers fan. While you may not be totally knowledgeable, you still know a great amount about them. Check out Harlee's Web site to learn more fun facts and increase your JoBros familiarity!

0-10 Correct: You are a casual fan of the Jonas Brothers. You might like to listen to the Jonas Brothers' music sometimes, but you don't know much about their personal lives. Don't worry though—the Jonas Brothers are still fans of their music's fans!

Answer key: 1. a, 2. c, 3. b, 4. d, 5. b, 6. a, 7. b, 8. a, 9. d, 10. b, 11. c, 12. a, 13. b, 14. b, 15. c, 16. b, 17. d, 18. c, 19. a, 20. b, 21. c, 22. a, 23. b, 24. d, 25. a, 26. c, 27. b, 28. b, 29. d, 30. b

Which Jonas Brothers are you?

Mostly A's: Kevin is your guy!

Mostly B's: Joe's the one for you!

Mostly C's: Nick is meant to be yours!

129

Kevin Jonas's Faves

I ♥ The Jonas Brothers

Joe Jonas's Faves

Nick Jonas's Faves

Song Scramble Crossword Puzzle

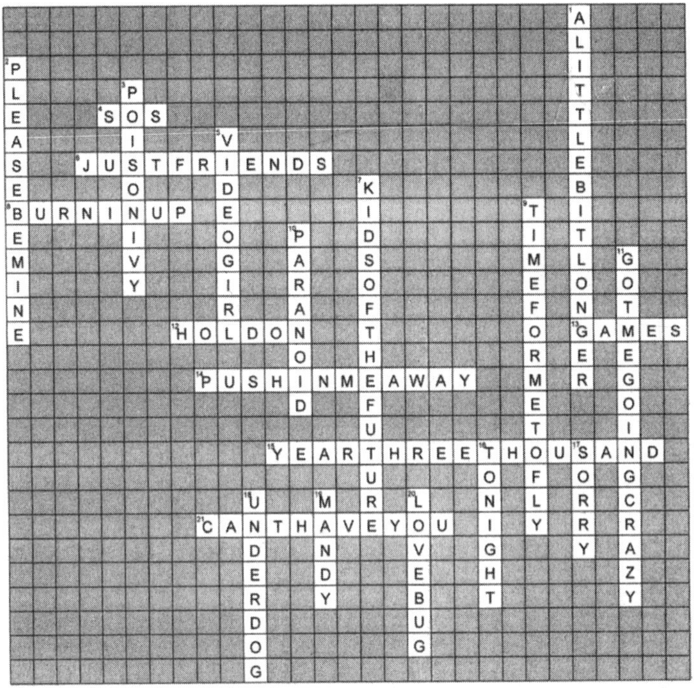
1 ALITTLEBITLONGER
2 PLEASEBEMINE
3 POISONIVY
4 SOS
5 VIDEOGIRL
6 JUSTFRIENDS
7 KIDSOFTHEFUTURE
8 BURNINUP
9 TIMEFORMETOFLY
10 PARANOID
11 GOTMEGOINGCRAZY
12 HOLDON
13 GAMES
14 PUSHINMEAWAY
15 YEARTHREETHOUSAND
16 UNDERDOG
17 SORRY
18 TONIGHT
19 MANDY
20 LOVEBUG
21 CANTHAVEYOU

Harlee Harte is a fictitious junior at Hollywoodland High School. She is the celebrity columnist for her school's student newspaper, where she writes the column "HarteBeat."